Unlocking Your Greatest Potential

I Will Rise And You Will Too

Unlocking Your Greatest Potential
2nd Edition

ISBN 979-8-9851441-5-4

Published by Conqueror Productions, LLC
Jacksonville, Florida

Acknowledgements

As I turn the pages of this incredible journey that culminated in "Unlocking Your Greatest Potential," I am filled with immense gratitude and appreciation for the wonderful souls who have been instrumental in bringing this workbook to life, embodying the "I Will Rise Mentality" throughout its creation.

Crystal, your unwavering support and insightful feedback have been a beacon of light, guiding me through the challenging moments and celebrating the triumphs. Your dedication to this project has not gone unnoticed, and I am truly grateful for your invaluable contribution.

Stacy, your meticulous attention to detail and your relentless pursuit of excellence have elevated I WILL RISE AND YOU WILL TOO to new heights. Your belief in the potential of this work has been a constant source of motivation, driving me to strive for nothing but the best.

Tony, your wisdom and public support have been a grounding force throughout this journey. Your ability to see the bigger picture and your willingness to share your knowledge have been instrumental in our growing phase of I WILL RISE AND YOU WILL TOO.

Ali, your creative spark and innovative ideas have infused this project with energy and excitement. Your passion for empowering others to unlock their greatest potential is both inspiring and contagious.

Robin, your patience and kindness have provided a safe space for ideas to flourish and grow. Your nurturing spirit and genuine care has left a lasting impact on both I WILL RISE and on me personally.

Acknowledgements

Dr. Diaz, your expertise and wisdom have been invaluable to the development of this workbook. Your dedication to fostering growth and transformation is truly admirable, and I am honored to have had you as a part of this journey.

Tami Jean, your encouragement and belief in the power of the "I Will Rise Mentality" has been a driving force behind this workbook. Your support has been a gift, and I am thankful for your unwavering faith in this project. Without you we would not be here. Thank you so much.

To my family, Trisha, Uncle Rick and Katie, I thank you for your unrelenting support . You have all been a well of knowledge and people I could turn to, to help build this booklet, as you are all on the same pursuit to make the world a better place. Thank you and I love you deeply.

Dr. Richard Erhardt, I deeply appreciate your discernment in guiding me through the writing process of this workbook. Your unwavering commitment has helped lay the very foundation on which this book was built.

To those who have supported me and believed in my journey, thank you from the bottom of my heart. Your encouragement and faith have been a beacon of light, guiding me through the highs and lows of this creative process. Your support has made all the difference, and I am deeply grateful for your unwavering belief in me and in the potential of this workbook.

This workbook is a testament to the power of collaboration, belief, and resilience. Thank you to each and every one of you who have been a part of this journey. Your contributions have been invaluable, and I am profoundly grateful for the role you have played in unlocking the greatest potential within these pages, and within me.

With heartfelt gratitude,

Olet

Table of Contents

Introduction - Embracing the 'I Will Rise' Mentality

Welcome to the **"I Will Rise And You Will Too"** workbook, a powerful guide designed to help you discover the best version of yourself and build the bridges to get there. This workbook is built upon four fundamental principles that form the bedrock of the "I Will Rise and You Will Too" mentality.

These principles are:

1.Being Encompassed in Gratitude: Gratitude is the cornerstone of positive empowerment. By recognizing and appreciating the positive aspects of life, even amidst adversity, we can find strength, hope, and a path to a brighter future.

2. Rooted in the Understanding That Life Is Challenging and That Is Okay: Life's challenges are a part of the human experience. Embracing this understanding allows us to navigate these challenges with resilience and grace.

3. Faith Without Works is Dead, and You Must Fall in Love With the Process of Becoming Great: Belief is the catalyst for change, but it's the action that propels us forward. This principle encourages us to combine faith with purposeful action, and to find joy in the journey of personal development.

4. Social Support And Mutual Aid One Person Helping Another Person Makes Both People Stronger: We are stronger together. Offering and receiving support from others not only strengthens our bonds but also amplifies our individual and collective strength.

Throughout this workbook, you will embark on a comprehensive exploration of these principles, each chapter focusing on a specific aspect of personal growth and empowerment. We will guide you and focus on internal redevelopment, understanding yourself, cultivating a positive mindset, and setting meaningful goals. These tools will help you build the bridges you need to get you from where you are to where you ultimately want to be.

By actively engaging with the exercises, reflections, and activities within these pages, you'll gain insights, develop resilience, and discover the power of mutual support. This workbook is your companion on the journey to becoming the best version of yourself, and it's based on the belief that you have the potential to rise and become great.

Are you ready to Rise? Let's begin.

Throughout this booklet you will find keys, they are random and follow their own journey, but they are there to help you discover and harness your strengths. By embracing the information within these pages you will unlock your greatest potential. Remember, growth is a continuous process, and this booklet will help you navigate the exciting path of self-discovery and positive transformation. Keep turning the pages, applying the keys, and embracing the possibilities that lead to the best version of yourself.

I Will Rise And You Will Too

Chapter I.

Discovering The Best Version of Yourself

In our fast-paced world filled with external distractions and constant demands, it's easy to lose sight of one of the most important journeys you can embark on—the journey to get to know yourself. This chapter delves into why it is crucial to explore the depths of your own being, your values, desires, strengths, and weaknesses. Getting to know yourself is not a self-indulgent act; it is the foundation upon which personal growth, self-empowerment, and authentic living are built.

The Importance of Self-Exploration:

Understanding who you are helps you gain clarity about your life's purpose and goals. This is a process. For some people, this process begins with finding their likes and dislikes. For others they may already know. Some people may like to go on adventures, do charity work or spend time with family. Other people may not have had the opportunity to find out what they like.

Do you have a clear understanding of what your values are, maybe your goals? The following worksheets are going to help you gain a clear sense of self, leading you to be more confident in your decisions. When you have a clear sense of self, you can make choices that align with your values and aspirations.

Part I: Clarity of Purpose

WHO AM I?

1. List Five Adjectives: Describe yourself using five adjectives (e.g., creative, thoughtful, determined, etc.)

_____

_____

_____

_____

2.Personal Values: Think about what matters most to you. List three values you hold dear and explain why (e.g., honesty, kindness, hard work, etc.).

_____

_____

_____

Mirror, Mirror on the Wall

3. Long-Term Goals: Write down three goals you want to achieve in the next year year.

2. Short-Term Goals: Write down three goals you want to achieve in the next few months that align with who you are and what you value.

GOALS

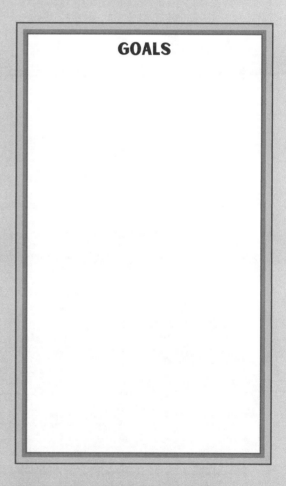

GOALS

Reflection

1. How do the adjectives you chose in (Who am I) relate and help you with your goals in (Mirror, mirror on the Wall) ?
• Answer:

———————————————————————

———————————————————————

———————————————————————

2. How do you think understanding yourself better help you in making decisions about your future?
• Answer:

———————————————————————

———————————————————————

———————————————————————

3. Do any of your goals not align with your values? If yes, think about why you chose them.
• Answer:

————————————————

————————————————

————————————————

Finding Your Keys
• Our keys are the strengths, passions, and skills we possess. Identifying them is the first step to unlocking our potential.

Part II: Authenticity

Authenticity is the key to meaningful relationships and a fulfilling life. When you know yourself, you can show up in the world as your true self, without pretense or masks. In a world where bullying and being judged is at an all time high, knowing who you are on the inside is more important than ever.

Understanding your authentic self is needed to navigate the roller coaster of life. Without understanding, you consequently show up as they want you to, instead of your authentic self. This leads to a potential life of confusion, anger and regret.

Objective: By the end of this worksheet, you should be able to understand the importance of authenticity and recognize how being genuine enhances relationships and overall life satisfaction.

Understanding Authenticity
1. Define Authenticity: In your own words, write a short definition of what you believe "authenticity" means.

2. List Three Traits of Authentic People: Think of someone you know who is genuine and authentic. What are three qualities or behaviors they display? (See examples below)

List 3 qualities of authentic people

1. ....

2 ....

3 ....

4 ....

Describe how those 3 qualities are displayed

1. ....

2. ....

3. ....

4. ....

Examples of authentic qualities

- Have realistic perceptions of reality
- Are accepting of themselves and of other people
- Are thoughtful
- Have a non-hostile <u>sense of humor</u>
- Able to express their emotions freely and clearly
- Are open to learning from their mistakes
- Understand their motivations

Self-Reflection

1. Moments of Authenticity: Recall a time when you felt you were truly yourself, without pretending or trying to fit in. Describe the situation and how you felt.

Situation:

Feelings:

2. Moments of Pretense: Recall a time when you felt you weren't being true to yourself, maybe trying to fit in or please others. Describe the situation and how it made you feel.

Situation:

Feelings:

The Impact of Authenticity on Relationships

1. Think of a relationship (friend, family, or other) where you feel you can be your true self. How does this authenticity impact the relationship?
• Answer:

2. Now, think of a relationship where you feel you can't be entirely authentic. What holds you back, and how does it affect the relationship?
• Answer:

Action Steps

1. **Small Steps to Authenticity:** List three things you can start doing to be more authentic in your daily life.
- a. _____
- b. _____
- c. _____

2. **Overcoming Barriers:** Identify one thing that often stops you from being authentic. Next to it, write down one strategy to overcome it.

Barrier: _____

Strategy: _____

Closing Thoughts: Authenticity is a journey, not a destination. By striving to be true to yourself, you pave the way for deeper connections and a more fulfilling life. Remember, the most genuine version of you is the best one!

Part III: Resilience

Objective: By the end of this worksheet, you should grasp the importance of resilience. In this you will learn to better understand your triggers, coping mechanisms, and emotional responses. The more self aware you become the better you can navigate life's challenges.

> **Resilience:** The capacity to <u>withstand</u> or to recover quickly from difficulties; <u>toughness</u>. the remarkable resilience of so many institutions"

Below you will find an example of resilience

Example: Helen Keller, a remarkable woman who overcame immense challenges, exemplifies the power of resilience. Born deaf and blind, she faced a world of silence and darkness. Yet, Helen did not let her disabilities define her. With the help of her teacher, Anne Sullivan, Helen developed a language of touch and learned to communicate through tactile sign language. This journey required immense resilience as she persisted through frustration and setbacks, ultimately breaking through the barriers that seemed insurmountable.

Helen Keller's resilience extended beyond communication. She pursued education at Radcliffe College, becoming the first deaf-blind person to earn a bachelor's degree. Her determination and resilience not only transformed her own life but also inspired countless others, proving that with unwavering perseverance, one can triumph over seemingly insurmountable odds and contribute meaningfully to society.

1. **Examples: List three examples of resilience from your own life or from the lives of people you admire.**

- **Importance: Why do you think resilience is important?**

Building Resilience

1. Challenges: Describe a current challenge you are facing.

2. **Strategies:**
List three resilience strategies you can apply to overcome this challenge.
Some resilience strategies include:
-Developing a strong support network,
-Practicing mindfulness,
-Setting realistic goals, and maintaining a positive outlook.

3. Reflection: Reflect on how using the strategies from the previous exercise makes you feel, and how it might change the outcome.

Feelings:	Possible Changes in outcome:

4. **Positive Thinking: List three positive affirmations that you can use to motivate yourself during tough times.**
- **a)** _____
- **b)** _____
- **c)** _____

5. **Support System: Identify three individuals in your life who provide support and encouragement.**
- **a)** _____
- **b)** _____
- **c)** _____

Reflecting on Resilience

1. **Growth:** In what ways have you grown as a result of overcoming past challenges?

_____

_____

_____

2. **Learning:** What have you learned about yourself through the process of building resilience?

_____

_____

_____

3. **Future Application:** How will you apply early on what you've learned about resilience to future challenges?

_____

_____

_____

Identifying Triggers

1. List Your Triggers: Think about situations, people, or events that may cause you stress or strong emotional reactions. List three of them.

Trigger: something that causes someone to feel upset and frightened because they are made to remember something bad that has happened in the past

Recognizing Emotional Responses

1. Describe an Emotional Response: Recall a recent situation where one of your triggers was activated. Describe the situation and note how you felt.

Situation:

Emotional Reaction:

Are you happy with your response? If not, what could you have done differently?

---

2. Reflection on Emotions: How do you usually handle strong emotions? Do you tend to act on them, reflect on them, or suppress them?

Coping Mechanisms

    A coping mechanism is a way your mind handles difficult situations or stress. It's like a tool your brain uses to manage tough feelings or challenges. Coping mechanisms can be helpful because they allow you to deal with problems in a healthier way, making it easier to face and overcome tough situations.

    These mechanisms can vary from person to person and might include activities like talking to friends, practicing mindfulness, or engaging in hobbies. By using coping mechanisms, individuals can better navigate stress, anxiety, or other emotions, promoting mental well-being. Developing a repertoire of effective coping strategies can enhance resilience and make it easier to cope with the ups and downs of life. It's important to discover what works best for you and to cultivate a range of coping mechanisms for different situations.

Coping Mechanisms

1. List Your Coping Strategies: Think about the ways you deal with stress or challenges. List three strategies or activities that help you cope.

- a. _____
- b. _____
- c. _____

2. Evaluating Effectiveness: Which of your coping strategies do you feel is the most effective? Why?
- Answer:

_____

_____

Building Resilience Through Self-Awareness

1. Improving Coping Mechanisms: Think of one new coping strategy you'd like to try the next time you face a challenge.

- New Strategy:

_____

_____

_____

_____

2. Staying Aware: How can you remind yourself to be self-aware and use these coping strategies when faced with challenges?
• Answer:

_____

_____

Closing Thoughts: Building resilience doesn't happen overnight. It's a journey of understanding yourself, recognizing your reactions, and finding ways to cope with challenges. Remember, the better you know yourself, the stronger you'll be in the face of adversity.

Finding Your Keys
Like a master key, self-awareness can open numerous doors. Reflect on who you are and who you want to become.

Part IV: Strengths and Weaknesses

We all have unique strengths and weaknesses that shape our abilities and limitations. Identifying and utilizing our strengths can contribute to our sense of purpose and achievement, while acknowledging and working on our weaknesses can lead to personal growth.

◆ What activities or tasks do you excel at effortlessly, without feeling much strain or effort? List at least three things that come naturally to you.

◆ What are some projects that energize and engage you, leaving you feeling fulfilled and satisfied?

◆ What are some challenges or problems that you consistently find easier to tackle compared to others?
Think about situations where you seem to excel in problem-solving.

Strengths

◆ In what situations do you find yourself providing guidance or support to others?

◆ What aspects of your personality or character contribute positively to your relationships or interactions with others?

◆ When reflecting on past experiences, which moments or accomplishments stand out as your strengths?

Weaknesses

1.In what situations do you feel overwhelmed or stressed?

2.Are there any areas where you frequently receive negative feedback from others?

3.Are there any habits or patterns of behavior that you recognize as detrimental or unproductive?

Weaknesses

4. What are some weaknesses or challenges that you tend to compare yourself to others in?

5. Do you struggle with setting boundaries or saying no to others' requests?

6. When working in a team, what roles or responsibilities do you struggle with?

Vision Board

1. Vision Board: On a separate piece of paper, create a vision board. Use pictures, words, and drawings to represent your dreams, goals, and what you want your life to look like in the future.

A vision board is a visual representation of your goals, dreams, and aspirations. It typically consists of a collage of images, words, and affirmations that reflect what you want to achieve in various areas of your life, such as career, relationships, health, or personal development. The purpose of a vision board is to serve as a powerful tool for manifestation and motivation. By creating a visual display of your goals, you're reinforcing them in your mind and focusing your attention on what you want to attract into your life. Regularly viewing your vision board can help inspire and remind you of your objectives, fostering a positive mindset and encouraging proactive steps toward achieving your aspirations.

Your Vision Here

I Will Rise And You Will Too

Having embarked on the journey of self-discovery, we've cultivated a vision that's uniquely ours. It's akin to discovering a treasure trove of dreams, talents, and hidden strengths. Now, the inevitable question arises: "What do I do with all this newfound knowledge about myself?" It's crucial to understand that while this treasure of self-awareness has immense value, it's just the beginning. The journey from self-awareness to self-actualization is where the real work and magic happen.

As we set out on this path, it's essential to be mindful that there will be a multitude of things to learn. The terrain might sometimes seem unfamiliar or challenging. But remember, every great quest is filled with lessons, and it's these lessons that form the narrative of our growth. The process may occasionally feel overwhelming, but it's not daunting. Think of it as a grand adventure, where every step, no matter how small or uncertain, is a leap towards realizing the best version of ourselves. Every stumble, a lesson; every challenge, an opportunity.

But how do we navigate this journey? Just as a craftsman requires tools to create masterpieces, we need tools to build the bridges that will connect our present to our envisioned future. These tools—strategies, mindsets, habits, and actionable steps—are what we will delve into in the upcoming chapters. As we equip ourselves with these tools, the path to where we want to go becomes clearer, and the 'I Will Rise' mentality transforms from a hopeful sentiment to an actionable roadmap.

Chapter II. Encompassed In Gratitude

    Amid life's swirling storms and towering challenges, a resolute voice within us proclaims, "I Will Rise And You Will Too." At the core of this tenacity is a profound sense of gratitude. "Gratitude: The Gift of Perspective" leads our exploration, highlighting how a heartfelt appreciation can shift our view, making mountains appear as molehills. As we delve into "Using Gratitude to Combat Past Trauma," we uncover gratitude's transformative power to heal and offer solace for wounds once thought permanent. Finally, "Turning Traumas into Triumphs" brings to the forefront inspiring tales of those who, with gratitude as their compass, have transformed their deepest pains into their greatest strengths.

Unlocking Doors
Behind each door lies an opportunity, a lesson, or a challenge. Not all doors are easy to open; some may require a combination of keys.

Gratitude: The Gift of Perspective

Gratitude is a powerful emotion that reminds us of the good things in life. Think of it as a spotlight that shines on moments, people, and experiences that bring joy, comfort, and meaning to our lives. While it's easy to get caught up in the challenges and stresses of everyday life, feeling grateful helps us refocus on what truly matters. It's like pausing to admire the beauty of a sunset or the sound of a loved one's laughter. These moments, though simple, can have a profound impact on our overall well-being and happiness.

At times, it can be difficult to feel grateful, especially when we face hardships or setbacks. But it's during these challenging moments that gratitude can be most transformative. When we choose to look beyond our immediate struggles and acknowledge the good around us, we gain perspective. We start to see our problems as temporary, and we recognize that there are always reasons to be thankful, no matter how small. This shift in mindset can lead to increased resilience, optimism, and a stronger sense of purpose.

Building a habit of gratitude doesn't require grand gestures. It can be as simple as jotting down three things you're thankful for every day, or taking a moment to express appreciation to someone who's made a difference in your life. Over time, these small acts can create a ripple effect, not just in our own lives but in the lives of those around us. After all, gratitude is contagious. When we share our thankfulness with others, we inspire them to do the same, creating a cycle of positivity and appreciation.

Objective: Understand the benefits of gratitude and learn how to cultivate it in daily life to enhance well-being and happiness.

1.Describe a recent moment or event where you felt grateful, and why.

2.List three emotions or feelings you associate with this grateful moment.

Recognize the Benefits

1. How did expressing or feeling gratitude affect your mood or perspective?

2. Can you recall a time when gratitude helped you through a challenging situation? Describe briefly.

Daily Gratitude Practice

List three things you are grateful for today.

today

Unlocking Doors
• Fear is a lock. Courage is the key. Confront what holds you back, and you'll find doors opening more easily.

MAKE *Today* Great

2. Write a short gratitude post card to someone who has made a positive impact in your life.
(You can choose to send it or keep it as a personal reflection.)

POSTCARD

Building Bridges
• Bridges connect us to new horizons and possibilities. They represent the paths we create to move past obstacles and challenges.

Setting Gratitude Goals

1. What is one way you can incorporate gratitude into your daily routine?

2. Name an activity or practice (e.g., journaling, meditation) that can help you focus on gratitude regularly.

Sharing Gratitude

1. List two people you would like to express gratitude to this week.

2. Describe a way you can show appreciation to someone in your community or workplace.

_____

_____

Note: Remember, gratitude is a journey, not a destination. It's about recognizing the good in life, big or small. As you continue to cultivate gratitude, you'll find it becomes a natural and uplifting part of your daily routine.

Part II: Using Gratitude to Combat Past Trauma

Everyone goes through tough times, and for some, these experiences can be really traumatic. It's like carrying a heavy backpack filled with bad memories and feelings. However, one tool to help lighten this load is gratitude. Gratitude is all about focusing on the good things in our lives and being thankful for them. When we stop and think about what we're grateful for, it's like adding balloons to our backpack. These balloons don't make the bad memories disappear, but they can help lift our spirits and make the weight feel a little lighter.

Now, you might wonder, "How can being thankful help with bad memories?" When we face trauma, our minds often replay those painful moments, making us feel stuck or sad. But when we practice gratitude, we give our minds a positive job to do. Instead of playing those hurtful memories on repeat, we can remind ourselves of the good things, like a friend's kindness, a fun day out, or even our favorite song. By doing this regularly, we train our brains to see the brighter side of things, which can make it easier to deal with the tough stuff.

Lastly, practicing gratitude can make us stronger in the long run. Just like how exercising helps our muscles grow, being thankful helps our emotional strength grow. Over time, as we keep focusing on the good things, we build up resilience. This means that even if new challenges come our way, we're better prepared to face them. So, while gratitude can't erase trauma, it's a powerful tool that helps us heal, grow, and find happiness even after tough times.

gratitude CHANGES every thing

Objective: To explore the role of gratitude in healing from past trauma, understanding its benefits, and practicing gratitude-focused activities.

Section 1: Understanding Gratitude and Trauma
1. Definitions-

• Gratitude: _____

• Trauma: _____

2. Reflection: How do you think gratitude can help in overcoming trauma?

_____

_____

_____

_____

_____

_____

_____

Benefits of Gratitude

1. List the benefits of practicing gratitude:
   (Use personal understanding)

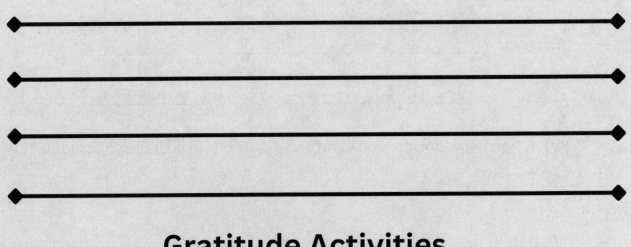

Gratitude Activities

1. Gratitude Journal: Write down three things you're
   grateful for today and why.

2. Gratitude Letter:

Think of someone who has supported you through your tough times. Write a thank-you note to them. You don't have to send it, but writing it can help you appreciate the support you've received.

Lets Reflect

1. How did practicing these gratitude activities make you feel?

◇—————————————————◇

◇—————————————————◇

◇—————————————————◇

2. How can you incorporate gratitude into your daily routine to support your healing journey?

◇—————————————————◇

◇—————————————————◇

◇—————————————————◇

◇—————————————————◇

Note: Healing from trauma is a complex process. Gratitude is one of many tools that can be beneficial. Always consult with a therapist or counselor when addressing past trauma.

Overcoming Negative Thoughts

Overcoming negative thoughts requires a conscious effort to change patterns of thinking and develop a more positive outlook on life. Negative thinking can stem from various sources, including past experiences, low self-esteem, or ongoing stress. To combat these thoughts, it's essential to first become aware of them. Pay attention to your inner dialogue and notice when negative thoughts arise. Challenge these thoughts by asking yourself whether they are based in reality, and try to find evidence that contradicts them. Practice positive affirmations and remind yourself of your strengths and achievements. Additionally, engage in activities that bring you joy and surround yourself with supportive people. Remember, changing thought patterns takes time, but with consistency, it is possible to cultivate a more positive mindset.

Awareness:
Write down three negative thoughts you've had recently.

-
-

-

2.Challenge the Thoughts:

   • For each negative thought, ask yourself: "Is this thought based in reality?" or is it an opinion you made yourself? Or is it a fear that has consumed you and is now a reality?

3.   Positive Affirmations:

   • For each negative thought, write a positive affirmation.
   • Example: If the negative thought is "I am not good enough," the positive affirmation could be "I am worthy and capable."

Take a problem that you are are going through and have struggled to get past. Imagine If a friend came to you with this problem, what advice or comfort would i offer them?

Dear,

Reflection:

- At the end of the week, reflect on how the previous exercises affected your thought patterns.
- Did you notice a change in your negative thoughts?
- What strategies were most helpful for you?

VISUALIZATION

1. WHEN VISUALIZING, CONNECT YOUR EMOTIONS WITH YOUR THOUGHTS. IF YOU'RE THINKING ABOUT SUCCESS, DO NOT JUST LET IT BE A THOUGHT... THINK OF WHAT IT FEELS LIKE AND ALLOW YOURSELF TO BE THERE.

2. IN THIS SPACE, THINK OF A MOMENT FROM YOUR PAST WHERE YOU FELT IMMENSE GRATITUDE. RELIVE THAT MOMENT, FOCUS ON THE FEELINGS AND SENSATIONS.

3. CLOSE YOUR EYES AND IMAGINE A SAFE SPACE WHERE YOU FEEL COMPLETELY RELAXED AND SECURE.

Part III: Turning Trauma into Triumph

Life is full of ups and downs, and everyone at some point experiences moments of pain and trauma. These experiences, whether big or small, can leave deep emotional scars and sometimes hold us back from pursuing our dreams or leading a fulfilling life. However, with the right mindset and tools, we can transform our past traumas into stepping stones towards a brighter future. Instead of viewing traumatic experiences as permanent roadblocks, we can see them as lessons that shape our character and teach us resilience.

Using trauma as a stepping stone involves reframing our perspective. It means looking beyond the pain and seeing the strength that emerged from it. For instance, someone who has faced a lot of rejection in life might develop an unparalleled determination to succeed. Another person who has faced loss might cultivate deep empathy and compassion for others. By focusing on these positive traits and growth that came from adversity, we can harness the energy from past traumas to fuel our drive and ambition. It's about recognizing that our past does not define us, but rather equips us with unique tools and insights that can be invaluable in our journey forward.

Of course, healing from trauma takes time, and it's essential to seek support when needed, whether it's from friends, family, or professionals. As we work through our past experiences, we can also set clear goals for the future and identify the skills and strengths we've gained from our past. Over time, we'll find that the very challenges that once seemed insurmountable can become the foundation upon which we build our dreams. By embracing our history and using it as a catalyst, we can transform our trauma into triumph.

Objective: Understand how to transform past traumas into tools for personal growth and success.

Reflect on Past Trauma
What is one of your favorite stories when a person took their trauma and turned it into triumph?

Lets talk about Trauma

1. Describe a traumatic event or experience from your past.
*Note: Write briefly without going into distressing detail.

2. List three emotions or feelings you associate with this experience.

●

●

●

Identify Growth and Strengths

3. What skills or strengths did you develop or discover as a result of this experience?(e.g., resilience, empathy, determination)

_____

_____

_____

4. Were there any lessons or insights you gained from this trauma?

_____

_____

_____

Reframing Perspective

5. Write a short statement describing how you might view this trauma as a stepping stone rather than a roadblock.

6. List three positive actions or steps you can take moving forward, using the strengths or lessons identified on the "Identify and Growth" Worksheet

7. What is one long-term goal influenced by the strengths or lessons you've identified?

Seek Support

1. List two people or resources you can reach out to for support or guidance.

1. _____

2. _____

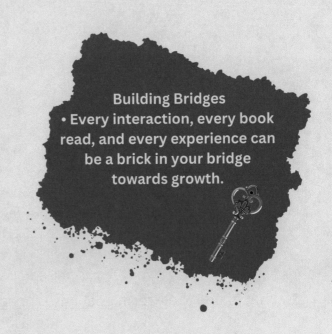

Building Bridges
• Every interaction, every book read, and every experience can be a brick in your bridge towards growth.

Note: Remember that healing is a journey, and it's okay to seek professional help or counseling to process traumatic experiences. This worksheet is a tool to help frame your perspective, but it's essential to prioritize your mental and emotional well-being.

Chapter III.
Rooted in the Understanding That Life Is Challenging and That's Okay

The Importance of Shifting Perspective:

Embracing the "I Will Rise And You Will Too" mentality is rooted in acknowledging the natural hurdles of life and viewing them as opportunities rather than setbacks. Challenges are inevitable; however, our perspective on them profoundly shapes our reactions and outcomes. By actively working to shift our viewpoint, this mindset helps us to tackle problems head-on, believing that we can get through them and come out even stronger.

Having the perspective that life is difficult and that's OK can be a transformative way of viewing the world. Firstly, this mindset fosters resilience. When we anticipate and accept that challenges are an inherent part of our journey, we are not blindsided by them. Instead, we face them with a sense of preparedness, understanding that these hardships are not unique to us but a shared human experience. Rather than getting bogged down by problems, we become adept at navigating through them, knowing that they're just a chapter in our larger story.

Furthermore, this understanding can lead to a deeper sense of contentment. By setting realistic expectations about life's nature, we can better appreciate the good times and find strength during the tough ones. We're less likely to be overwhelmed by the pursuit of constant perfection or the illusion of a problem-free existence. Recognizing that everyone, no matter how their life may seem on the surface, faces difficulties, we develop empathy and a sense of community. We learn to value our experiences, both good and bad, as they shape our character and teach us valuable lessons. In embracing life's challenges, we not only find personal growth but also connect more authentically with those around us.

Mentorship: The Key makers
• In our journey, we'll come across individuals who've crafted keys we've never seen. Learn from them, and add their wisdom to your keyring.

Worksheet: Shifting Your Perspective with the "I Will Rise And You Will Too" Mindset

Reflect on a Recent Challenge:
1. Describe a recent situation or event that felt challenging or overwhelming.

2. Initial Reactions:
List three feelings or thoughts you experienced during this challenge.

3. Universal Experiences:
Write down two instances where you've seen or heard of someone else facing a similar challenge.

4. Growth Opportunities:

List three lessons or skills you can learn from facing this challenge.

5. Affirmations for Resilience:

Create three positive affirmations to remind yourself of your strength and capability.

1. "I am _____."
2. "I can _____."
3. "I will _____."

6. Future Perspective:

Imagine yourself six months from now. How do you hope to view this challenge in hindsight?

Accepting Your Starting Point

Living our best life doesn't mean waiting for perfect circumstances but rather optimizing what we currently possess. This proactive approach stems from a foundation that appreciates life's highs and lows, recognizing that every experience, good or bad, contributes to our growth and evolution. It's not about sidestepping difficulties but about transforming them into bridges that will lead us to a more fulfilled life.

It's important to understand that everyone's starting point is unique, and it's perfectly alright if it's not where we envisioned it to be. What truly matters is not where we begin, but our commitment to growth, learning, and lifting ourselves up from that point. By accepting our current position, we give ourselves permission to move forward without unnecessary burdens, confident in the knowledge that every step we take is a step towards progress and betterment.

Worksheet:
Understanding Your Starting Point and Building Towards Your Goals

Recognizing and understanding our starting point is crucial in charting a path towards our aspirations. The "I Will Rise And You Will Too" mentality reminds us that while life presents challenges, we have an inherent strength to face them and come out stronger. This worksheet aids in gaining clarity on where we stand, what we wish to achieve, and the tools and support available to us. With a clear roadmap and a ready mindset, we are better equipped to journey towards our goals.

Mastering Your Keys
- It's not enough to merely possess keys. We must hone them, refine them, and use them wisely.

Where Are You?

Below is an exercise about where you are in terms of your goals, the feelings associated with it, and the perceived challenges that you are going to face in trying to accomplish them.

Understanding where you are in terms of your goals, including the associated feelings and perceived challenges, is vital for several reasons. Firstly, it promotes self-awareness, helping you recognize and manage the emotions tied to your objectives. This emotional awareness can guide your actions, enabling you to make decisions that align with both your goals and your well-being.

Additionally, understanding the perceived challenges allows you to anticipate obstacles and develop strategies to overcome them. This proactive approach increases your preparedness and resilience in the face of difficulties, making it more likely that you'll stay on course despite potential setbacks.

1. Self-Reflection: Your Starting Point   Example

Describe where you currently are in terms of your goals, feelings, and challenges.

Goals?

weight loss-i want to lose 20 pounds

Feelings?

overwhelming,

Challenges?

no one in the house eats healthy

Self-Reflection: Your Starting Point

Use the work sheet below with one goal, feeling, and express the challenges you may face. Write the answers in detail. If you want to do this with other goals you can use a separate sheet of paper and continue the exercise.

Where Are You?

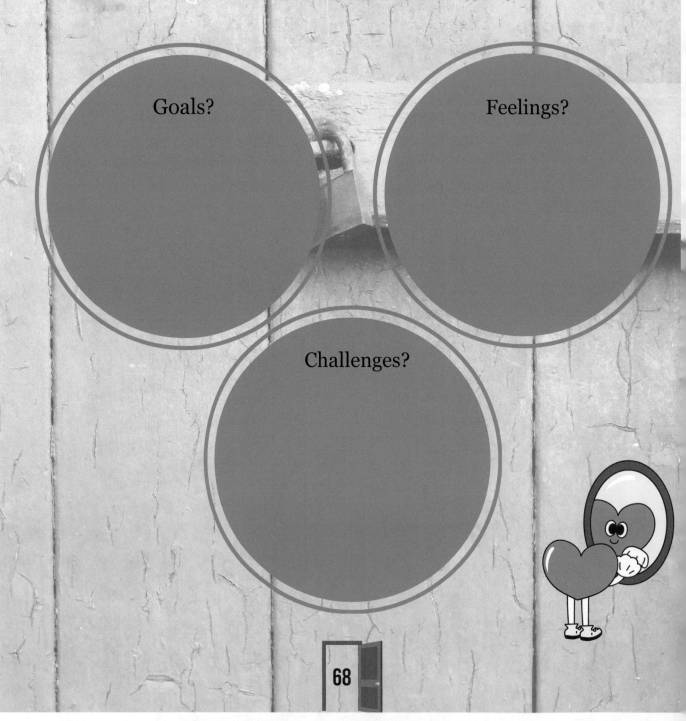

Goals?

Feelings?

Challenges?

2. Past Achievements

•List Two things you've accomplished or overcome in the past that you're proud of. This will help you recognize your resilience and capabilities.

3. Defining Your Goals

• Clearly state two primary goals you want to work towards.

Mastering Your Keys
• Each challenge faced and door unlocked sharpens our keys, making the next challenge easier to overcome.

4. Barriers and Challenges

• Identify potential barriers or challenges you might face in achieving each of the above goals.

1. Barrier for Goal 1: _____

2. Barrier for Goal 2: _____

3. Barrier for Goal 3: _____

Tools and strategies are like your secret weapons for reaching your goals. They help you stay organized, focused, and on track. Tools can be anything from apps on your phone to simple things like a to-do list or a calendar. They make it easier to keep track of what you need to do and when. Strategies are like game plans. They're the steps you take to make sure you're using your time and energy wisely. For example, setting small goals that you can reach one step at a time or figuring out the most important tasks to do first. When you use the right tools and strategies, you'll be better equipped to tackle challenges and make your goals a reality.

5. Tools and Strategies

• For each barrier listed above, identify a tool or strategy you can use to overcome it.

1. Strategy for Barrier 1: _____

2. Strategy for Barrier 2: _____

3. Strategy for Barrier 3: _____

6. Support System

List three individuals or groups that can support you in your journey and how they might help.

Create three daily affirmations to boost your confidence and reinforce the "I Will Rise And You Will Too" mentality.

1. "I am _____ and I believe in my journey."

2. "Every challenge brings _____ to my life."

3. "Everyday I am becoming_____ and closer to my dreams."

Build A Foundation With A Strong Moral Compass

Building a strong foundation to become the best version of yourself requires a strong moral compass and acceptance of a fundamental truth: life is challenging, and that's perfectly OK. This understanding, rather than being a source of discouragement, can actually be the bedrock upon which personal growth is built. To cultivate this foundation, one must practice regular self-reflection, acknowledging both achievements and areas of improvement without judgment, and accepting that our starting point is neither good nor bad, but just where we are, and that's okay.

To build a foundation on being the best version of yourself you need to have a moral compass that is built on strong values that guide how you act and think. Think of honesty like a rulebook—it keeps you truthful and helps others trust you. Hard work reinforces our commitment to excellence teaching us the value of persistence and discipline in the face of challenges. Your character is like your personal brand; it's made up of your good traits and doing the right thing even when no one's watching. These are the principles that your foundation should be built on, and a start to a good moral compass.

Acceptance statement:

Write a short paragraph accepting where you are right now in your journey. Using your moral compass, share how your new foundation will help you in the process of becoming the best version of yourself.

Chapter IV. Faith Without Works is Dead and You Must Fall in Love With the Process

Part I: Combining faith and action

At the heart of the "I Will Rise And You Will Too" mentality, lies an unshakable faith in not only a greater purpose, but also in one's ability to overcome adversities. However, faith on its own is not enough. Just as the word is written, "Faith without works is dead," (King James, 2:17) it is essential to back up our beliefs with tangible actions. A dream remains but a figment of imagination unless paired with effort. Similarly, wanting to become great, to rise above challenges, demands more than just the desire. It requires dedication, and a passionate commitment to the journey. It is crucial to fall in love with the process of becoming great, not just the end result.

Setting goals and creating timelines is a part of this journey. These act as markers, guiding our steps and providing direction. But, as with any journey towards greatness, there will be moments of stress, pressure, and pain. These are natural companions of progress and growth, reminding us that greatness often comes at a price. They test our resolve, and it's during these times that our faith and works merge. It's the intersection where we decide to either retreat in the face of adversity or to push forward with even more determination. Sometimes, the weight of our ambitions can be intimidating, leading to fear and doubt. Yet, it's essential to remember that it's okay to feel scared. Fear is a natural emotion, but it shouldn't be the determining factor in whether we pursue our dreams or not. If you can't shake off the fear, the mantra should be with faith: "Do it scared."

In essence, the journey to greatness is a blend of faith, action, and an unwavering commitment to the process. While challenges are inevitable, they are also the forge upon which our character is shaped and refined. By setting clear goals, being realistic about the challenges ahead, and maintaining the "I Will Rise And You Will Too" mindset, we not only navigate the hurdles but also use them as bridges to create a pathway to success. Whether you're driven by passion, purpose, or sheer willpower, remember that the process, with all its highs and lows, is what truly defines greatness.

Guardians of the Gate
• Sometimes, our biggest challenges aren't locked doors but guardians who stand in our way. They represent our fears, doubts, and insecurities.

Objective: The worksheet below aims to help you blend your faith with practical steps, creating a harmonious path toward self-improvement and personal growth.

Faith, whether it's in a religious context or a broader sense of belief, can offer individuals a source of strength during challenging times. Believing in something larger than oneself can provide comfort, hope, and resilience, helping people navigate difficulties with a sense of purpose and endurance.

Faith often comes with a set of values and principles. Integrating these into one's life can serve as a moral compass, guiding decision-making. Whether through religious teachings or personal beliefs, faith can contribute to a sense of direction and purpose, helping individuals make choices aligned with their core values.

It's important to note that the role of faith varies from person to person, and what works for one may not work for another. It's a deeply personal aspect of self-help that individuals can choose to incorporate based on their beliefs and experiences.

1. Personal Definition: In your own words, describe what your faith means to you.

2. Key Teachings: List 3 essential teachings or principles from your faith that inspires and guides you.

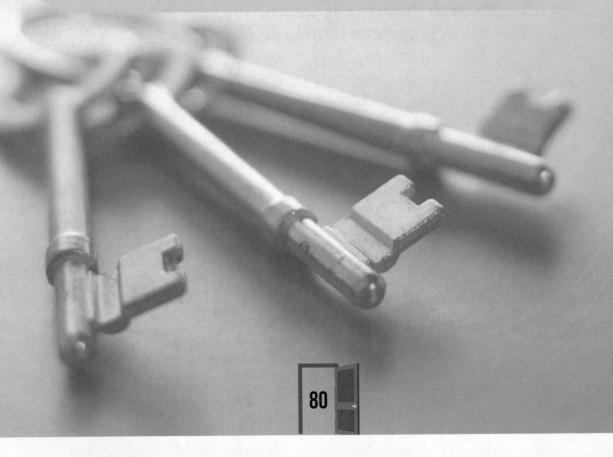

What is a vision?

A vision is the ability to think about or plan the future with imagination or wisdom.

1. Vision for Yourself: Imagine a vision is a distant place that you hope to be at in ten years from now. What does that look like to you. Use four words that best describe this future position

2. Actionable Steps: using actions and the four words write some specific steps you plan to take in the near future that will help you get to that future position..

3. Accountability Partner: Identify someone from your community or circle whom you can share your goals with to keep you accountable.

Merging Faith and Action

1. Daily Reflection: Create a daily practice, like prayer or meditation, where you reaffirm your commitment to combining your faith with action. Describe it below.

2. Overcoming Challenges: Anticipate a challenge you might face in your journey and suggest a strategy for overcoming it.

Challenge:_____
_____
_____

_____
_____

Strategy:_____
_____
_____
_____

Part II: Falling In Love With The Process

Becoming the best version of yourself is not just about reaching a destination; it's about embracing the journey. Each step, no matter how small, is a piece of the puzzle that makes up the larger picture of who you want to become. Falling in love with the process means appreciating the challenges as much as the victories, understanding that setbacks are just setups for greater comebacks. It's about recognizing growth in every moment, being patient with oneself, and celebrating small wins along the way. When you truly fall in love with the process, you find joy in the everyday grind, making the path to self-improvement not just a task, but a passion.

Guardians at the Gates
• Conversing with the guardians, understanding their concerns, and proving your growth can lead to them stepping aside.

1. Define Your Why: Before diving into any task, understand why you're doing it. What motivates you? What's the deeper reason behind your goal?

- My Goal: _____
- My Motivation: _____
- Type your reasons below..

_____

_____

_____

_____

Micro Goals

Let's say your overall goal is to improve your fitness. A micro goal related to this could be to walk or jog for 15 minutes every day this week. This smaller, achievable goal is a stepping stone toward your larger fitness objective. It's specific, measurable, and can help you gradually build the habit of regular exercise, making the larger goal more manageable and realistic.

2. Set Micro-Goals: Instead of just big goals, set smaller ones along the way. What are some mini-goals you can celebrate? Use the main goal you listed on the previous exercise.

• Micro Goal 1: _____

• Micro Goal 2: _____

• Micro Goal 3: _____

3. Journal Your Journey: Spend a few minutes each day or week to jot down what you learned, felt, and experienced.
• Below, write down this week's highlights of what you learned, felt and experienced.

The Power of Collective Bridges
• While personal growth is a solo journey, building bridges with others amplifies our potential. Collaboration can lead to bridges stronger and longer than anything we could build alone.

4. **Reflect on Challenges:** Instead of avoiding difficulties, reflect on them. What challenges did you face? What did they teach you?

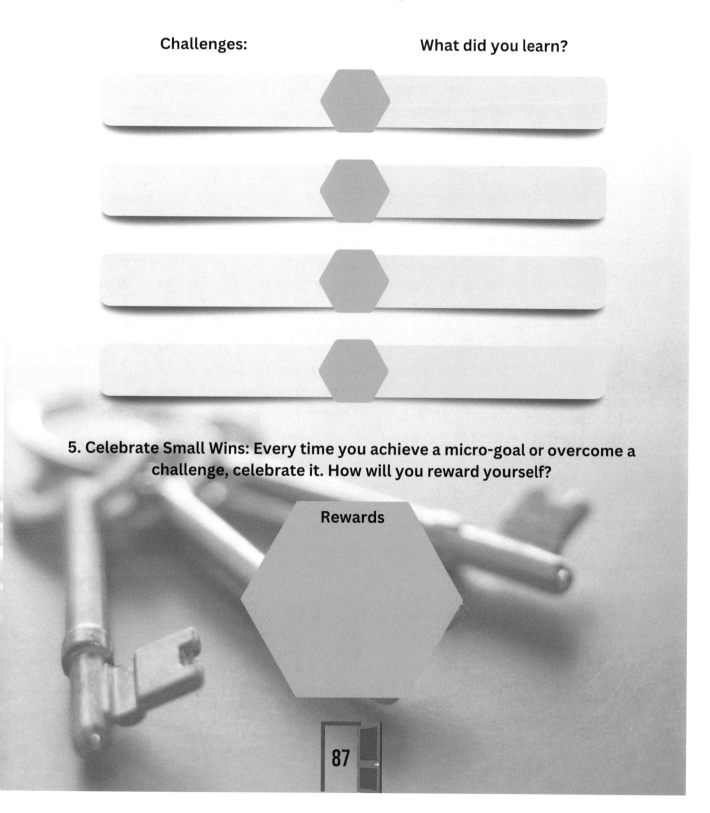

Challenges: What did you learn?

5. Celebrate Small Wins: Every time you achieve a micro-goal or overcome a challenge, celebrate it. How will you reward yourself?

Rewards

Are you falling in love with the process yet?

For some you may be excited, you're learning things about yourself that you don't even know and with this new information you can take on a lot more. For others, falling in love with the process does not even seem possible, and the things that you learned may leave you feeling more overwhelmed. Everybody's journey is different. I want to assure you that the greatest version of ourselves is in reach. You making it this far is incredible, and the best is yet to come!!

In the previous worksheets and chapters before we have learned more about ourselves. With that information, you should have created a vision of who you would like to be and where you would like to go. You learned you can use your past as tools to help build your future. We spoke about setting goals, large and small, to help make your path clear as possible.

In this process you are going to learn that people are your greatest resource. Knowledge is powerful but we can not do it alone. On the next worksheet you will be asked to find a person close to you and share with them a goal you are trying to accomplish and the progress you need to make. The purpose of this is to get honest feedback and be held accountable to your own expectations.

The Infinite Doors
• **The journey of self-improvement never ends. There's always another door, another bridge, and another key to craft.**

6. Feedback Loop: Ask someone you trust for feedback on a goal you are trying to work on. Do this over a week span and check back to see what they think of your progress. What did they notice? How can you improve?

What is the goal you are working on and who did you ask?

Feedback received?

How can you improve?

By regularly using this worksheet, you can keep track of your progress, understand the value of each step, and truly fall in love with the process of becoming the best version of yourself.

Worksheet: Embracing the Process Amidst Challenges

Pressure Points

• List three areas or tasks that currently cause you stress or discomfort.

1

2

3

1.The Value of Pain and Pressure

• For each point above, write down one potential growth opportunity.
Example:
Pressure point-Relationship becoming a step dad
Growth- Patience, learning to be a better leader, having more empathy

1. Growth from Point 1: _____

2. Growth from Point 2: _____

3. Growth from Point 3: _____

2. Combatting Fear

• Describe a situation where fear might hinder your progress.

3. Strategies to "Do It Scared"

• Remember that fear should not be a determining factor as to whether or not we continue down the path of becoming our best selves.

Below write down three methods or reminders to help you push through fear.

"A GOAL WITHOUT A PLAN IS JUST A DREAM."
The Basics Of setting and completing your goals

What is my Goal_____   Goal Start Date_____

Steps to reaching my Goal

Things that will help me Complete my Goal

I Will Know I Have Reached Goal Because:

Goal Completion Date _____

Chapter V. Social Support and Mutual Aid
One Person Helping Another Person Makes Both People Stronger

The "I Will Rise And You Will Too" mentality encapsulates the power of mutual benefit and the importance of community. This philosophy is grounded in the understanding that our individual successes are deeply interconnected with the well-being of those around us. Within a community, members benefit from a diverse array of skills, knowledge, and experiences. When individuals support one another, they access a collective pool of resources far richer than any single person could gather. This camaraderie ensures that challenges faced by one can be tackled with the collective wisdom of many, magnifying individual strengths while providing a safety net for shared vulnerabilities.

Resources in such a community extend beyond tangible assets to include shared experiences, advice, connections, and emotional backing. Embracing the "I will rise, and you will too" philosophy means that knowledge, tools, and opportunities circulate generously and purposefully among community members. This collaborative approach guarantees everyone has the tools they need to prosper, reinforcing the idea that personal progress and community welfare are tightly interwoven. In such an environment, the acts of elevating others become integral to the journey towards personal success.

This worksheet is designed to help you recognize and appreciate the benefits of mutual aid and social support. By reflecting on their experiences, identifying ways to offer and seek support, and understanding the interconnection between personal success and community welfare. Through this exploration, you'll realize that the collective strength of a community amplifies the power and potential of each of its members.

Worksheet: Understanding the Power of Mutual Aid and Social Support

The Ripple Effect

Think of a situation where you helped someone else. Did their progress or happiness influence you in return? Describe.

Reflect on Personal Experiences

Recall a time when someone supported or helped you. How did it make you feel? How did it affect your situation?

Mutual Aid in Action

List three ways you can actively support someone in your community this week.

96

Benefits of Social Support

• Write down three benefits you gain when you're part of a supportive community.

_____

_____

_____

Strengthening Ties

• Identify two relationships or connections you'd like to strengthen and list steps to nurture those bonds.

1. **Relationship/Connection:** _____
    Steps:_____

_____

2. **Relationship/Connection:** _____

Steps: _____

_____

The Strength in Unity

Describe in your own words the essence of "I Will Rise And You Will Too" and how it applies to community and mutual aid.

Setting an Example

Think about how your actions can inspire others to adopt the "I Will Rise And You Will Too" mentality. What steps can you take to be a role model?

Here are some benefits of Mutual Aid and Social Support:

Shared Learning: When one person teaches another, both get a chance to understand the topic better. The one teaching reinforces what they know, and the one learning gains new knowledge.

Boosted Confidence: Helping others can make you feel good about yourself. And when someone helps you, it reminds you that people care about you. Both feelings can boost your confidence.

Teamwork Makes Tasks Easier: Two people working together can often get things done faster and better than one person alone. It's like when you and a friend clean up together; it's quicker and more fun!

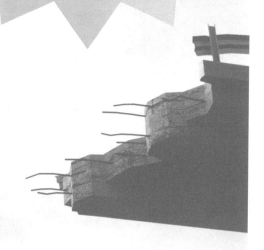

Here are some benefits of Mutual Aid and Social Support:

Emotional Support: Knowing someone has your back can make tough times easier to handle. And when you support someone else, you learn to understand and care for others better.

New Perspectives: When we help each other, we can see problems and solutions in new ways. Your friend might have a different way of looking at things, and together, you can come up with even better ideas.

Together, these reasons show that when we support and help each other, everyone benefits and grows stronger.

Conclusion

The philosophy of "I Will Rise And You Will Too" is anchored in four principles: Being encompassed in gratitude. Rooted in the understanding that life is challenging and that's okay. It's built on the foundation that faith without works is dead and you must fall in love with process. It comes to fruition under social support and mutual aid; one person helping another makes both people stronger.

Initiate this journey with gratitude. This isn't merely about appreciating major achievements; it's also about valuing the nuanced experiences and minor victories that shape our daily lives. Next, it's crucial to understand that life's difficulties are universal. They aren't personalized roadblocks designed to hinder us, but rather, they are tests of our resilience and adaptability.

Merely having faith or positive intentions, while commendable, won't propel us forward on their own. Concrete actions, commitment, and persistent effort are the cornerstones of tangible progress. It's similar to preparing for an academic or athletic challenge—the consistent dedication and work behind the scenes lead to eventual success.

Lastly, the journey of self-improvement isn't a solitary one. Mutual aid underscores the power of collective effort. When one individual supports another, it's a dual-faceted gain, fortifying both the giver and the receiver.

In summary, the "I Will Rise And You Will Too" mindset is a holistic approach to personal growth. By integrating these principles, not only does an individual pave their path to excellence, but they also inspire and uplift those around them.

Conclusion: The Grandest Version
• As you continue to unlock doors and build bridges, always remember that the grandest version of yourself is not a final destination, but a continuous journey.

Spiritual

Financial

BUILDING BRIDGES

Mental Health

105

Physical Health

Building Bridges

By this time you should have a better understanding of where your starting point is and where you want to be. What we now want to do is close that gap, and build a bridge between those areas. How will we do that?

In this activity we have taken your journey and sectioned it into four areas in your life. Spiritual, Financial, Mental health and Physical health. The reason we are doing this is to take what can seem to be a daunting process and make it much more manageable. You will use the information that you have gained throughout the workbook as well as your personal life to figure out the questions you need to ask yourself. Everyone's journey is unique and therefore the questions you need to ask yourself should be tailored around how YOU can build your bridges.

Spiritual

Objective: In a couple paragraphs answer the two questions below. The purpose of this exercise is to help you gain an understanding of your overall situation.

Where are you spiritually right now and why?

Where do you want to be?

Spiritual

Objective: Now that you have an understanding of where you are and why, and where you want to be. Lets figure out how far along our bridge is built so we can see what is needed to finish this construction. So you can continue on your path to living your best life.

How far along is your bridge built?
Fill in the planks below

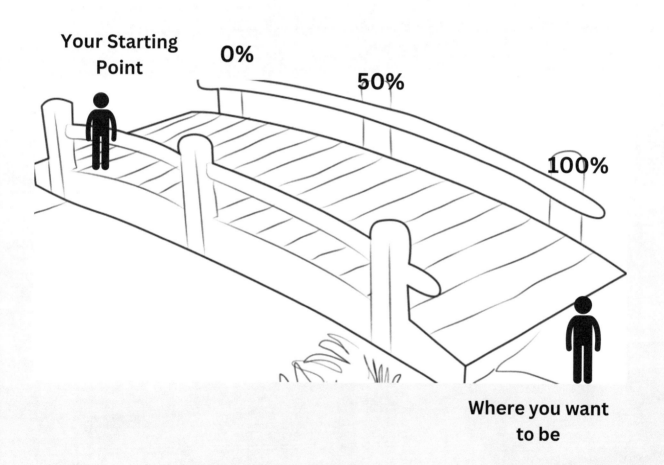

Your Starting Point

0%

50%

100%

Where you want to be

Spiritual

Before we continue I want you to know that some of the hardest steps have already been taken. Once you create a vision and understand where you are at in that vision, you can then start to ask yourself the questions that need to be answered in order for you to grow.

Example: Olet is working on this exercise
Olet's starting point: Confused about what I should and should not believe.
Where Olet wants to be: To be confident in what I believe to give it a real chance to better my life.
Bridge: Olet feels his bridge is about 50% built and is now ready to work on the other 50%
*** Olet is now at the Q&A section which is where you currently are. Here are the questions and answers he gave.
Olet's Q&A:
Q: What do I need to know to make this decision?
A: Study religion, practice its teachings for a period of time.

Objective: Below there is a Q&A that only YOU can create because your journey is unique and no one knows it but you. With the understanding of where you are and where you want to be ask yourself some questions that can help bring clarity to what some of your next steps should be.

Your Q&A

Q: _____

A: _____

_____

Spiritual

Q: _____

A: _____

_____

_____

Q: _____

A: _____

_____

_____

What micro goals need to be put in place to accomplish those answers?

Using the answers from the Q&A above we are now going to create some manageable micro goals that will bring the answers to fruition and complete the bridge to the best version of yourself.

Example: Olet's answers to his Q&A were:
- Study religion
- Practice its teachings for a period of time

What are some goals he will need to put in place to accomplish those answers?

Micro Goals:
- Figure out which religion I want to start with
- How long is a period of time.

Spiritual

Your Goals

What micro goals do you need to put in order to get the results to build the bridge?

Micro Goals:

_____

_____

_____

_____

Financial

Objective: In a couple paragraphs answer the two questions below. The purpose of this exercise is to help you gain an understanding of your overall situation.

Where are you financially right now and why?

Where do you want to be?

Financial

Objective: Now that you have an understanding of where you are and why, and where you want to be, lets figure out how far along our bridge is built so we can see what is needed to finish this construction. Then you can continue on your path to living your best life.

How far along is your bridge built?
Fill in the planks below

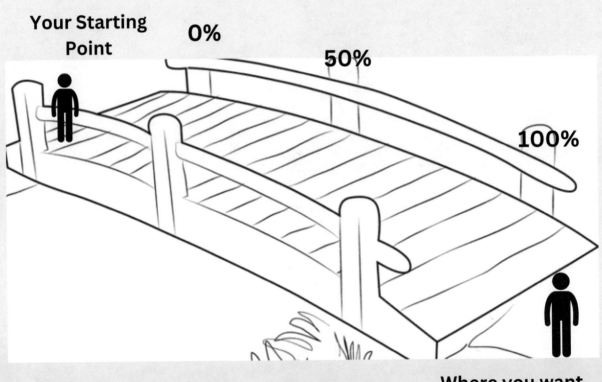

Your Starting Point

0%

50%

100%

Where you want to be

Financial

Before we continue I want you to know that some of the hardest steps have already been taken. Once you create a vision and understand where you are at in that vision, you can then start to ask yourself the questions that need to be answered in order for you to grow.

Example: Crystal is working on exercise

Crystal's starting point: Doing okay at the moment. Some debt. Room for improvement.

Where Crystal wants to be: Debt free.

Bridge: She feels her bridge is about 75% built and is now ready to work on the other 25%

*** Crystal is now at the Q&A section which is where you currently are. Here are the questions and answers she gave.

Crystal's Q&A:

Q: What changes do I have to make to become debt free?

A: Higher more dependable drivers, Work harder, Set more boundaries

Objective: Below there is a Q&A that only YOU can create because your journey is unique and no one knows it but you. With the understanding of where you are and where you want to be ask yourself some questions that can help bring clarity to what some of your next steps should be.

Your Q&A

Q: _____

A: _____

_____

_____

Financial

Q: _____

A: _____

_____

_____

Q: _____

A: _____

_____

What micro goals need to be put in place to accomplish those answers?

Using the answers from the Q&A above we are now going to create some manageable micro goals that will bring the answers to fruition and complete the bridge to the best version of yourself.

Example: Crystal's answers to her Q&A were:
- Higher more dependable drivers
- Work harder
- Set more boundaries

What are some goals she will need to put in place to accomplish those answers?

Micro Goals:
- Do better screening of the individual before hiring.
- Do more research before taking loads. Risk vs Reward
- Set boundaries between family and business

Financial

Your Goals

What micro goals do you need to put in order to get the results to build the bridge?

Micro Goals:

_____

_____

_____

_____

Mental Health

Objective: In a couple paragraphs answer the two questions below. The purpose of this exercise is to help you gain an understanding of your overall situation.

Where is your mental health right now and why?

Where do you want to be?

Mental Health

Objective: Now that you have an understanding of where you are and why, and where you want to be. Lets figure out how far along our bridge is built so we can see what is needed to finish this construction. So you can continue on your path to living your best life.

How far along is your bridge built?
Fill in the planks below

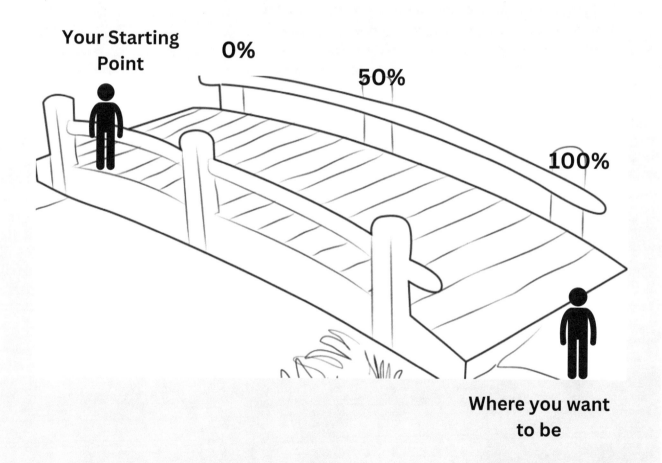

Your Starting Point

0%

50%

100%

Where you want to be

Mental Health

Before we continue I want you to know that some of the hardest steps have already been taken. Once you create a vision and understand where you are at in that vision, you can then start to ask yourself the questions that need to be answered in order for you to grow.

Example: Tami is working on this exercise.

Tami's starting point: Lives in Michigan. This causes her some mental struggles.

Where Tami wants to be: In Florida

Bridge: She feels her bridge is about 30% built and is now ready to work on the other 70%

*** Tami is now at the Q&A section which is where you currently are. Here are the questions and answers she gave.

Tami's Q&A:

Q:What does she need to do to move to Florida?

A: Save money, find a good school district, is transferring jobs an option?

Objective: Below there is a Q&A that only YOU can create because your journey is unique and no one knows it but you. With the understanding of where you are and where you want to be ask yourself some questions that can help bring clarity to what some of your next steps should be.

Your Q&A

Q:

A:

Mental Health

Q: _____

A: _____

_____

_____

_____

Q: _____

A: _____

_____

_____

What micro goals need to be put in place to accomplish those answers?

Using the answers from the Q&A above we are now going to create some manageable micro goals that will bring the answers to fruition and complete the bridge to the best version of yourself.

Example: Tami's answers to her Q&A were:
- Save money,
- Find a good school district,
- Is transferring jobs an option?

What are some goals she will need to put in place to accomplish those answers?

Mirco Goals:
- Each paycheck put away $100
- Narrow down top 10 school districts in Florida
- Email HR at workplace to see if there are transfers available.

Mental Health

Your Goals

What micro goals do you need to put in order to get the results to build the bridge?

Micro Goals:

_____

_____

_____

_____

Physical Health

Objective: In a couple paragraphs answer the two questions below. The purpose of this exercise is to help you gain an understanding of your overall situation.

Where is your physical health right now and why?

Where do you want to be?

123

Physical Health

Objective: Now that you have an understanding of where you are and why, and where you want to be. Lets figure out how far along our bridge is built so we can see what is needed to finish this construction. So you can continue on your path to living your best life.

How far along is your bridge built?
Fill in the planks below

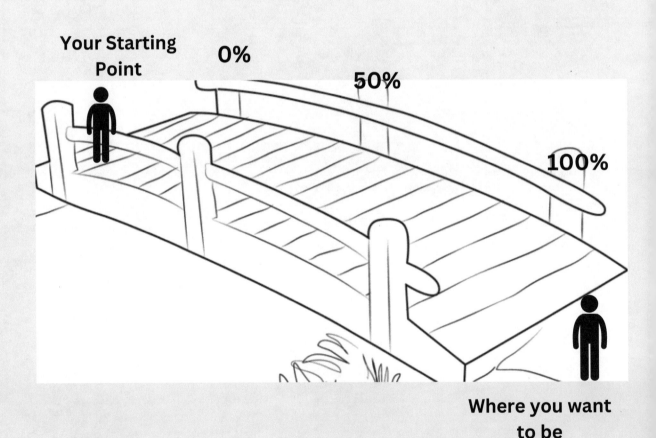

Your Starting Point

0%

50%

100%

Where you want to be

Physical Health

Before we continue I want you to know that some of the hardest steps have already been taken. Once you create a vision and understand where you are at in that vision, you can then start to ask yourself the questions that need to be answered in order for you to grow.

Example: Ali is working on this exercise.

Ali's starting point: Weight loss journey. Uncomfortable in body. Dr stated she is medically obese.

Where Ali wants to be: Comfortable in body, not medically obese.

Bridge: She feels her bridge is about 25% built and is now ready to work on the other 75%

*** Ali is now at the Q&A section which is where you currently are. Here are the questions and answers she gave.

Ali's Q&A:

Q: How can I mentally prepare for this weight loss journey?

A: Meet with Dr. and Keep a journal

Objective: Below there is a Q&A that only YOU can create because your journey is unique and no one knows it but you. With the understanding of where you are and where you want to be ask yourself some questions that can help bring clarity to what some of your next steps should be.

Your Q&A

Q:

A:

Physical Health

Q: _____

A: _____

_____

_____

Q: _____

A: _____

_____

_____

What micro goals need to be put in place to accomplish those answers?

Using the answers from the Q&A above we are now going to create some manageable micro goals that will bring the answers to fruition and complete the bridge to the best version of yourself.

Example: Ali's answers to her Q&A were:
- Meet with Dr.
- Keep a journal

What are some goals she will need to put in place to accomplish those answers?

Mirco Goals:
- Meet with PCP, inquire about a dietician.
- Reminder to write in the journal. Reflection and feelings on current self.

Physical Health

Your Goals

What micro goals do you need to put in order to get the results to build the bridge?

Micro Goals:

_____

_____

_____

_____

Dear Readers,

Congratulations!!!! You made it to the end of the workbook! Hopefully this is just the beginning of a new journey for you. There was a lot covered, so let me highlight just a few things.

1. Understand that your starting point is okay no matter where it is. The important part is to except it and be real with ourselves. Once we do that we are then able to better prepare for the journey ahead.

2. Life is a journey, don't get caught up with what others say and feel like you should be doing. Create a strong moral compass and let that be your guiding line along with a couple mentors. So many people think in permanence, they lose sight that the ebb and flows of life is what makes this world amazing.

3. Be grateful for everything in your life, the good and bad. It is hard to see but the bad can be incredible learning lessons that will lead you to live an amazing life. Never abuse people, even with work or people you don't particularly care for. If it is that bad separate yourself but never have the intention of just trying to get over in life. That thought process will cause you to fail in the long run. Life is about building, giving, and growing. If your thoughts do not align with that, the actions are just a temporary gain setting yourself up for a major setback.

4. Having a vision board done and a white board filled with goals to make that vision come into a reality, is one of the most pivotal actions that we need to take in order to create our dream life. When you have a vision it allows you to wake up and know what your purpose is. Journaling it all can help you sort out the emotions throughout the process . Be proud of accomplishing those micro goals and always give yourself timelines to keep track of it all.

5. The bridges concept at the end of the booklet was to make you aware that sometimes we just need to scale things down a bit. Piece by piece is how things are built. Sometimes we can work on certain areas of our life, then jump to another area. Eventually it will be complete, or at least that phase. The reality is we are ever evolving so its likely that once this bridge is built you will soon move on to the next one. So fall in love with the process....

Love y'all,
I WILL RISE AND YOU WILL TOO

About the Author

Emerging from a 15 year stint in maximum security prison, the author of "I Will Rise And You Will Too" has transformed his life and emerged as a beacon of inspiration and resilience. In the depths of his darkest moments, he forged the "I Will Rise" mentality, a powerful testament to the indomitable human spirit and the incredible potential for change and growth that lies within each of us.

Upon his release, the author seamlessly integrated back into society, turning his life around and dedicating himself to motivating others. Within a few years he traveled the nation and has established himself as a sought-after motivational speaker, sharing his transformative journey and the principles of the "I Will Rise" mentality.

His story is not just one of personal triumph, but a universal message of hope and empowerment, demonstrating that no matter where you find yourself in life, with determination, support, and the "I Will Rise And You Will Too" mindset you can rise above your circumstances and live the life you desire.

About the Editor

Tami Jean brings her own unique perspective and strength to "I Will Rise And You Will Too," serving as the editor and an invaluable supporter of the "I Will Rise" mentality. A survivor of domestic violence and a devoted single mom, Tami has triumphed over adversity and embodies the spirit of resilience and empowerment that the workbook promotes.

Her role in "I Will Rise" extends beyond the pages of the workbook, as she is a steadfast advocate for those who have experienced trauma, helping them realize that they too can overcome their challenges and live their best lives. With her keen editorial eye and deep personal understanding of the journey from survival to thriving, Tami has been instrumental in shaping the workbook into a powerful tool for change and transformation.

Together, the author and Tami Jean form a formidable team, united in their mission to inspire and empower others to rise, conquer their challenges, and live life to its fullest potential.

Made in the USA
Columbia, SC
04 February 2025

52533933R00076